HOW-TO LIBRARY

MAKING CLAY
BEAD CRAFTS

Written and Illustrated by Kathleen Petelinsek

CHERRY LAKE PUBLISHING • ANN ARBOR, MICHIGAN

CHERRY LAKE Publishing

Published in the United States of America by Cherry Lake Publishing
Ann Arbor, Michigan
www.cherrylakepublishing.com

Photo Credits: Page 4, ©vvoe/Shutterstock.com; page 5, ©hxdbzxy/
Shutterstock.com; page 6, ©Eugene Sergeev/Shutterstock.com; page 7,
©littleny/Shutterstock.com; page 29, ©Dragon Images/Shutterstock.com.

Library of Congress Cataloging-in-Publication Data
Petelinsek, Kathleen, author.
  Clay bead crafts / by Kathleen Petelinsek.
    pages cm. — (Crafts) (How-to library)
  Summary: "Complete fun craft projects using clay beads" — Provided by
publisher.
  Audience: Grades 4 to 6.
  Includes bibliographical references and index.
  ISBN 978-1-63137-777-8 (lib. bdg.) — ISBN 978-1-63137-797-6 (pbk.)
— ISBN 978-1-63137-837-9 (e-book) —ISBN 978-1-63137-817-1 (pdf)
  1. Beads—Juvenile literature. 2. Clay--Juvenile literature. 3. Handicraft--
Juvenile literature. I. Title.

TT860.P475 2014
745.58'2—dc23   2014001367

Cherry Lake Publishing would like to acknowledge the work of The
Partnership for 21st Century Skills. Please visit www.p21.org for more
information.

Printed in the United States of America
Corporate Graphics Inc.
July 2014

A NOTE TO ADULTS:
Please review the instructions for these craft projects before your children make them. Be sure to help them with any steps you do not think they can safely do on their own.

A NOTE TO KIDS:
Be sure to ask an adult for help with these craft activities when you need it. Always put your safety first!

HOW-TO LIBRARY

TABLE OF CONTENTS

The History of Bead Making

Beads can be made of wood, stone, clay, metal, glass, plastic, and many other materials.

People have been making beads and decorating with them for a very long time. Archaeologists have found beads from ancient civilizations all over the world. Unlike many items that archaeologists have uncovered, beads are not necessary for daily survival. You do not need beads to hunt for food or protect yourself from harsh weather.

In ancient times, beads were often used for decoration. They were also used in many other ways. Some ancient civilizations used beads as **currency** to trade for other items. Some used beads to show status or for religious purposes. Ancient Egyptians covered mummies with **intricate** beaded netting. In some cultures, beads were even believed to have protective or healing powers. Many ancient religions used beads for prayer, and some religions continue to do so today.

Early beads were made from shells, stones, seeds, animal bones and teeth, and even eggs. Glass and clay beads were made later.

Buddhism is one of many religions that use beads for prayer or chants.

Decorating with Beads

Beaded jewelry is easy to find in stores, but it is more fun to make your own!

Beads are found everywhere today. They are used to make many kinds of jewelry, including necklaces, earrings, and bracelets. Beads are also used to make key chains and belts, or even to decorate pillows, sweaters, or shoes. Today's beads are made of many different types of materials. They come in solid colors and patterns. They can be small or large. Beaded items may have just one bead or many beads.

Look around your home. Do you see something that can be decorated with beads? What kind of beads would you use?

Carry a sketchbook with you to draw your ideas. Ideas can come from anywhere. Maybe you see a bug with crazy spots. You could make a bead that looks like the bug! Perhaps the pull chain hanging from your ceiling fan would look fantastic with a large, decorative bead on the end. Sketching your ideas helps you plan out new kinds of beads and ways to string them together.

When you get an idea for a new project, make a sketch so you don't forget about it.

The Clay

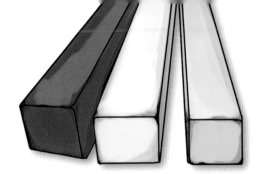

You can make your own bead designs by molding them out of clay. Modeling clay can be purchased at many hobby shops. There are two types of clays that you can buy in the store: air-dry clay and polymer clay. Air-dry clay is not as strong as polymer clay, but it does not require baking to harden it. Most types of polymer clay need to be baked in an oven before they harden. However, the final product is more durable than air-dry clay. There are several popular brands of clay available, including Sculpey, Kato, and Fimo. If you decide to use clay that requires an oven, ask an adult to help you follow the baking instructions on the package.

You can also make your own clay from some common household ingredients. Following are two recipes for making your own clay.

Simple Air-Dry Cornstarch Clay
This simple clay is easy to make and will work for most of the projects in this book.

Materials
- Saucepan
- Wooden spoon
- 1 cup water
- 1½ cups table salt
- 1 cup cornstarch
- Food coloring (optional)

Steps

1. Combine the water and salt in the saucepan.

2. Bring the water to a boil while stirring to dissolve the salt. Ask an adult to help you use the stove.

3. Once the salt is dissolved, remove the saucepan from the heat and quickly add the cornstarch. Stir until the mixture is sticky and stiff.

4. Stir in a few drops of food coloring if you want to make colored clay.

5. If you are not going to use the clay right away, store it in a sealed plastic bag in the refrigerator. Squeeze as much air as possible out of the bag before sealing it. This will stop the clay from drying out.

Homemade Air-Dry Polymer Clay

Not all types of polymer clay need to be baked in the oven. Create your own homemade air-dry polymer clay with this simple recipe.

Materials

- Nonstick pot
- Wooden spoon
- ¾ cup white glue
- 1 cup cornstarch
- 2 tablespoons mineral oil plus extra for removing it from the pot
- 1 tablespoon lemon juice
- Food coloring (optional)

Steps

1. Mix the glue and cornstarch together in the nonstick pot, using the wooden spoon.

2. Add the mineral oil and lemon juice. Blend well.

3. Ask an adult to help you cook the mixture over low heat. Stir constantly until the mixture resembles mashed potatoes.

4. Remove the pot from the heat.

5. When the clay is cool enough to touch, but still hot, squirt a small amount of mineral oil around the top of the clay. Use your hands to remove the clay from the pot. Ask an adult to help you.

6. **Knead** the clay until it is smooth. It is best to do this while the clay is still as hot as you can handle.

7. Knead in a few drops of food coloring if you want to make colored clay.

8. If you are not using the clay right away, store it in a sealed plastic bag in the refrigerator. Squeeze as much air as possible out of the bag before sealing it.

Creating Clay Beads

Now that you have bought or made clay, it is time to create some basic bead shapes that you can use for a variety of projects.

Materials

- Parchment paper
- Clay (store-bought or homemade)
- Clay tools
- Toothpicks
- Styrofoam block (if you are using air-dry clay)

Steps

1. Cover your work area with parchment paper to protect it.
2. Condition the clay by rolling and kneading it. You want the clay to be **pliable** and easy to work with.
3. Pinch off a small amount from the lump of conditioned clay to make your bead. The amount of clay you pinch off will determine your bead size. Try for a finished bead size with a **diameter** of ¼ inch (0.6 centimeters). Work the clay into your desired shape. You can make beads that are round, oval, heart-shaped, or any other shape you can think of. Use clay tools to help shape your clay.

4. If the bead is very soft when you are done shaping it, put it in the refrigerator for 10 minutes to firm it back up. That way it will not squish when you put a hole in it.

5. Pierce the bead with a toothpick to create a hole. Gently push and turn the toothpick like a drill until it pokes all the way through the bead.

6. If you are using air-dry clay, rest the hole of the bead on one end of the toothpick. Stick the other end of the toothpick into a slab of Styrofoam. Allow your beads to dry for 24 to 48 hours, until they are hard.

7. If you are using store-bought polymer clay, follow the directions on the package to bake your beads. Ask an adult for help with the oven.

Painting Your Beads

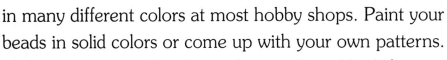

Now that you have some beads, it is time to paint them in a rainbow of colors. You can color your beads using acrylic paint, which is available in many different colors at most hobby shops. Paint your beads in solid colors or come up with your own patterns. Look at your sketchbook or take a walk and look for interesting color combinations if you need ideas.

Materials
- Old newspapers
- Dried or baked beads (*see pages 12–13*)
- Toothpicks
- Styrofoam block
- Acrylic paint
- Small paintbrushes
- Water for rinsing brushes
- Glossy polycrylic (optional)

Steps
1. Cover your work area with old newspapers.
2. Place a bead on the end of a toothpick. Then stick the other end of the toothpick into a Styrofoam block to create a stand to hold your beads as you paint.

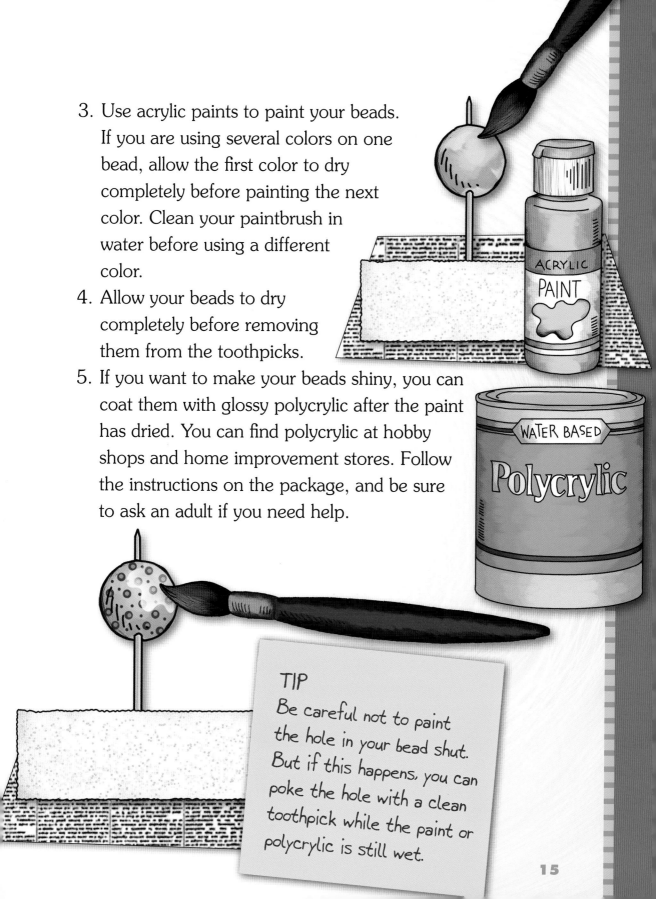

3. Use acrylic paints to paint your beads. If you are using several colors on one bead, allow the first color to dry completely before painting the next color. Clean your paintbrush in water before using a different color.

4. Allow your beads to dry completely before removing them from the toothpicks.

5. If you want to make your beads shiny, you can coat them with glossy polycrylic after the paint has dried. You can find polycrylic at hobby shops and home improvement stores. Follow the instructions on the package, and be sure to ask an adult if you need help.

TIP
Be careful not to paint the hole in your bead shut. But if this happens, you can poke the hole with a clean toothpick while the paint or polycrylic is still wet.

Simple Swirl Beads

You can mix colored clays to create crazy swirling patterns in your beads. Try a variety of different color combinations!

Materials

- Parchment paper
- Several different colors of clay (store-bought or homemade)
- Toothpick

Steps

1. Cover your work area with parchment paper to protect it.
2. Condition each color of clay by rolling and kneading it. The clay should be pliable and easy to work with.
3. Pinch off small pieces of clay from the lumps of conditioned clay colors. Roll them together into a bead that is about

the size of a large pea. Your bead will have swirls of different colors in it. You can use two colors or several colors.

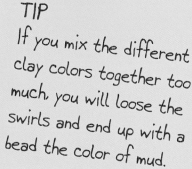

4. If the bead is very soft when you are done shaping it, put it in the refrigerator for 10 minutes to firm it back up. That way it will not squish when you put a hole in it.

TIP
If you mix the different clay colors together too much, you will loose the swirls and end up with a bead the color of mud.

5. Pierce the bead with a toothpick to create a hole. Gently push and turn the toothpick like a drill until it pokes all the way through the bead.

6. Make 15 to 20 beads.

7. Dry or bake the beads according to the directions.

8. Thread some beads onto a piece of string, then tie the ends together to make a bracelet!

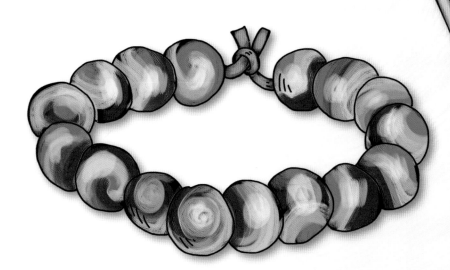

BFF (Best Friend's Fingerprint) Charms

Create these fun beads to make one-of-a-kind charms that you can give to your friends and family. They are perfect, personalized gifts!

Materials

- Parchment paper
- Clay (store-bought or homemade)
- Spoon
- Toothpick
- Old newspapers
- Acrylic paint in a variety of colors
- Paintbrushes
- Water for rinsing brushes
- Black acrylic paint
- Paper towels

Steps

1. Cover your work area with parchment paper to protect it.
2. Condition the clay by rolling and kneading it. The clay should be pliable and easy to work with.
3. Pinch off a marble-size piece from the lump of conditioned clay to make your bead.

4. Roll the clay into a ball and use a spoon to press it into a flat circle shape.
5. Press your fingerprint into the clay.
6. Make a second flat circle using the same method. This time, ask a friend to press his or her fingerprint into it.
7. Use a toothpick to poke a hole into the top center of each flattened circle.
8. Dry or bake the beads according to the directions.
9. Spread old newspapers on a work surface so you can paint your charm. Use your favorite color to paint the back of your bead. Allow it to dry. Once the back of the bead is dry, paint the front of the bead. Use your friend's favorite color to paint the back of his or her bead. Let it dry, and then paint the front side. Clean your paintbrush in water before using a different color.
10. Mix a small amount of black paint with water to make a very thin **glaze**. Paint the front of the charm with the glaze. Rub the surface lightly with a paper towel to remove the extra black paint from the top surface of the charm. The black coloring should remain inside the fingerprints.
11. Once the two charms are dry, you can string them together to make a necklace or bracelet that represents your friendship!

TIP

Make many charms so that you can make a necklace or bracelet for each of your friends!

Intricate Pressed Pendants

Create a large pendant with an interesting pattern pressed into it. You can use your pendant to make a necklace, decorate a key chain, or do anything else you can think of!

Materials
- Cutting board
- Parchment paper
- Colored clay (store-bought or homemade)
- Rolling pin or clay roller
- Metal charm
- Baby powder
- Clay tool knife
- Toothpick
- Glossy polycrylic (optional)

Steps
1. Cover the cutting board with parchment paper to protect it.
2. Condition the clay by rolling and kneading it. The clay should be pliable and easy to work with.
3. Pinch off a piece of clay that is about the size of a Ping-Pong ball.

4. Use the rolling pin or clay roller to flatten the ball of clay. The flattened clay should be about ¼ inch (0.6 cm) thick.

5. Coat the metal charm with baby powder to prevent it from sticking to the clay.

6. Gently press the charm into the clay until you make a pattern. Carefully remove the charm.

7. Use the clay tool knife to cut a shape out of the patterned clay. You can cut a circle, square, triangle, star, or any other shape that you like.

8. Use a toothpick to poke a hole into the top center of your shape.

9. Dry or bake the pendant according to the directions.

10. Coat your pendant with glossy polycrylic if you want it to be shiny.

11. Once your pendant is dry, you can use it to make a necklace or a key chain decoration.

Monogrammed Key Chain

Create a customized key chain with your initials stamped into it. Make a key chain for each member of your family so everyone will always know whose keys are whose!

Materials

- Cutting board
- Parchment paper
- Colored clay (store-bought or homemade)
- Rubber letter stamps of your initials
- Baby powder
- Clay tool knife
- Toothpick
- Glossy polycrylic (optional)
- Small jewelry clasp
- Key chain ring

Steps

1. Cover the cutting board with parchment paper to protect it.
2. Condition the clay by rolling and kneading it. The clay should be pliable and easy to work with.

3. Pinch off a piece of clay that is about the size of a Ping-Pong ball.

4. Roll the clay into a ball and flatten it with the palm of your hand.

5. Coat the letter stamps with baby powder to keep them from sticking to the clay.

6. Gently press the letter stamps into the clay and lift them off.

7. Use the clay tool knife to cut a shape out of the stamped clay. You can cut a circle, square, triangle, or any other shape that you like.

8. Poke a hole into the top of the circle of clay with the toothpick.

9. Dry or bake the clay according to the directions.

10. Coat your pendant with glossy polycrylic if you want it to be shiny.

11. Once your pendant is dry, attach a small jewelry clasp to the hole. Attach a key chain ring to the jewelry clasp.

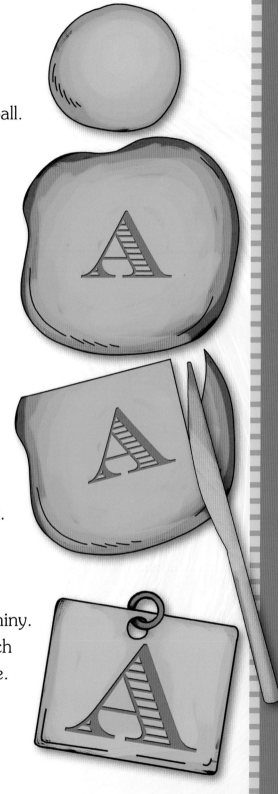

Spiral Cane Beads

Clay canes are **cylinders** of clay made with two or more colors. The canes are sliced to expose their unique, often intricate patterns.

Materials

- Cutting board
- Parchment paper
- Two colors of polymer clay (store-bought or homemade)
- Rolling pin or clay roller
- Sharp knife
- Toothpick

Steps

1. Cover the cutting board with parchment paper to protect it.
2. Condition each color of clay by rolling and kneading it. The clay should be pliable and easy to work with.
3. Pinch off a piece that is about the size of a Ping-Pong ball from one of the colors of clay.
4. Roll the clay ball flat using the rolling pin or clay roller. It should be about $1/16$ inch (0.2 cm) thick.

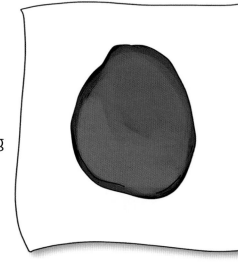

5. Repeat steps 3 and 4 with the other color of clay.
6. Stack one color of flattened clay on top of the second color.
7. Cut the two layers into a rectangle.
8. Gently roll the two colors together with your hands to form a cane.
9. Continue to roll the multicolored cane back and forth with your hands to press the clay layers together. Eliminate any air gaps between the layers.
10. Place the clay cane in the refrigerator for 30 to 60 minutes.
11. Pick one of the two colors to make the main color of the bead. Pinch a grape-size piece from the lump and roll it into a ball. Set it to the side.
12. Once the clay cane is firm, ask an adult to help slice off the end of the cane with a knife so the edge is clean.
13. Make a slice that is about $\frac{1}{8}$ inch (0.3 cm) thick. Repeat six times.
14. Place each slice of the cane around the ball. Once all six are placed, gently roll the ball with your hand to press the clay pieces together and make the ball smooth.
15. Use a toothpick to poke a hole through the swirly bead.
16. Dry or bake the bead according to the directions.

Watermelon Cane Beads

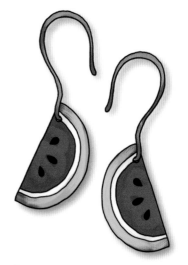

These colorful beads look like slices of juicy watermelon.
Use them to create fun, wacky jewelry!

Materials

- Cutting board
- Parchment paper
- Red, green, and white polymer clay
  (store-bought or homemade)
- Rolling pin or clay roller
- Sharp knife
- Toothpick
- Fine-point permanent black marker
- Glossy polycrylic (optional)

Steps

1. Cover the cutting board with parchment paper to protect it.
2. Condition each color of clay by rolling and kneading it.
   The clay should be pliable and easy to work with.
3. Pinch off a piece that is about the size of a grape from
   the lump of red conditioned clay.

4. Roll the red clay into a cylinder. It should be about 1 inch (2.5 cm) long and ½ inch (1.3 cm) in diameter. This shape is also called a cane.

5. Pinch off a smaller amount from the lump of white conditioned clay. Roll it flat using the rolling pin or clay roller. It should be about $^1/_{16}$ inch (0.2 cm) thick.

6. With help from an adult, use the knife to trim the left and right edges of the clay to be the same width as the length of the red clay cane.

7. Wrap the flattened white clay around the outside of the red clay cane.

8. Repeat steps 5 through 7 with the green clay.

9. Gently roll the multicolored cane back and forth with your hands to press the layers together. Make sure there are no air gaps between the layers.

10. Place the clay cane in the refrigerator for 30 to 60 minutes.

11. Ask an adult to help slice off the end of the clay cane so the edge is clean.

12. Slice a piece from the cane that is about ⅛ inch (0.3 cm) thick. Make a second cut across the slice to form two half-circle pieces.

13. Repeat step 12 until you have several half-circle slices.

14. Use the toothpick to poke a hole into the top of each slice.

15. Dry or bake the beads according to the directions.

16. Use a fine-point permanent black marker to draw small watermelon seeds on your beads.

17. Coat your watermelon slices with glossy polycrylic if you want them to be shiny.

TIP
You can make earrings out of your watermelon beads. If you want to make post earrings, you do not need to poke a hole into the beads before drying or baking them. You can simply glue the post right to the back of the finished bead.

Inspiration Is Everywhere

There are endless possibilities for making and decorating beads. In this book, you have learned a few methods of creating beads. You have learned how to make simple painted beads and swirled beads using colored clays.

You have also learned that you can press items into clay to create patterns. Can you think of other things that you can press into clay

Take a closer look at the things around you to get new ideas for craft projects.

to create patterned beads? Nature is full of interesting objects, including shells, dried leaves, and flowers. They can all help you make exciting new kinds of beads!

You have also learned how to make simple clay canes and turn them into beads. What other patterns can you create in a cane? How can you make these patterns into beads? Use your sketchbook to create and plan your ideas. Beads are small, but keep your ideas big!

Glossary

currency (KUR-uhn-see) a form of money

cylinders (SIL-uhn-durz) shapes with flat, circular ends and sides like the outside of a tube

diameter (dye-AM-uh-tur) a straight line through the center of a circle, connecting opposite sides

glaze (GLAYZ) a thin coat of liquid that is applied to pottery to give it a shiny, colorful finish

intricate (IN-tri-kit) complicated or containing many small parts or details

knead (NEED) to press, fold, and stretch dough with your hands to make it smooth

pliable (PLYE-uh-buhl) easily bent or shaped

For More Information

Books

Ross, Kathy. *Beautiful Beads*. Minneapolis: Millbrook Press, 2010.

Speechley, Greta. *Bead Crafts*. New York: Gareth Stevens Publishing, 2010.

Web Sites

The Crafty Crow—Bead Crafts

www.thecraftycrow.net/bead-crafts/

Do you enjoy working with beads? Visit this site for tons of projects with a variety of types of beads.

Lines Across—Polymer Clay for Beginners

www.linesacross.com/2012/09/polymer-clay-for-beginners-9-simple.html

This site offers some clay craft tips and projects, including bead creations.

Index

About the Author

Kathleen Petelinsek is a children's book illustrator, writer, and designer. As a child, she spent her summers drawing and painting. She still loves to do the same today, but now all her work is done on the computer. When she isn't working on her computer, she can be found outside swimming, biking, running, or playing in the snow of southern Minnesota.